WITHDRAWN

Spotlight on

Arms
and Armour

Tim Wood

Franklin Watts
London · New York · Sydney · Toronto

© 1989 Franklin Watts
Franklin Watts
12a Golden Square
London W1R 4BA

Franklin Watts Australia
14 Mars Road
Lane Cove
NSW 2066

Phototypeset by Lineage, Watford.
Printed in Hong Kong

UK ISBN: 0 86313 804 7
Illustrations: Jim Marks, Jeff Burn, John James/Temple Art

Photographs: Paul Forrester, The Photographers' Library, The Bridgeman Art Library, Robert Harding

Design: Edward Kinsey

Note: A number of the illustrations in this book originally appeared in *Arms and Armour, An Easy-Read Fact Book.*

Contents

The first weapons	4
The first armies	6
Greek and Roman soldiers	8
The Vikings	10
Knights	12
Archers	14
Knives and swords	16
The first cannons	18
Pistols	20
Rifles	22
Machine guns	24
The modern soldier	26
Unusual weapons	28
Arms and armour facts	30
Glossary	31
Index	32

The first weapons

Bronze Age people making weapons.

The first people used sticks and stones to kill animals and to fight each other. Later, Stone Age people learned how to make axes, knives and arrow heads from flint. Then about 5,000 years ago, humans discovered the secret of making metal weapons. At first they used copper but this was rather soft. They found that by adding a little tin to the copper, they could make bronze, a stronger metal. Iron was discovered in about 1,000 BC. Iron weapons were sharper and tougher than weapons made of bronze.

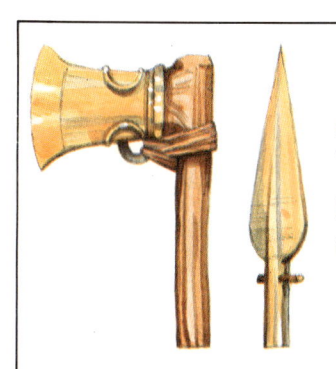

A bronze axe and spear.
The bronze was melted and poured into moulds. When the metal was cold and hard, the weapons were polished and sharpened.

The first armies

An Egyptian foot soldier walking beside a chariot.

6

Early soldiers fought in small groups and on foot. The Ancient Egyptians had the first armies. Their soldiers carried wooden shields covered with leather. They used spears, clubs and bronze swords or daggers. Most Egyptian soldiers fought on foot, but some rode in chariots. These were light carts with two wheels. One soldier controlled the horses, the other soldier threw spears or shot arrows.

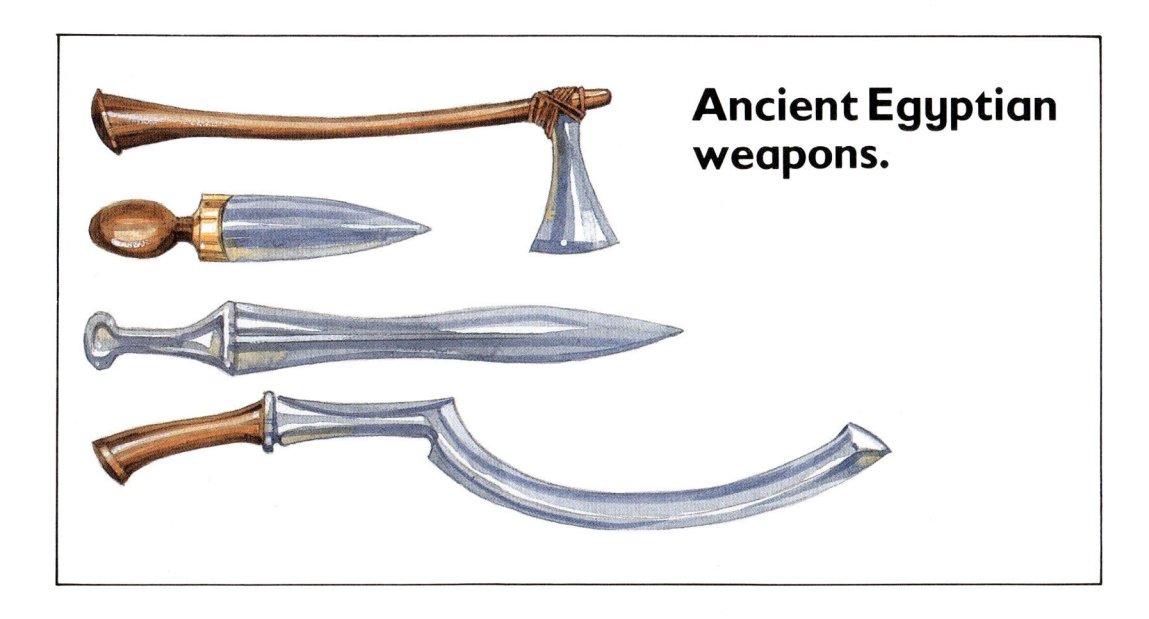

Ancient Egyptian weapons.

Greek and Roman soldiers

A Greek hoplite.　　A Roman legionary.

The soldiers of **Ancient Greece** were known as hoplites. Their weapons and armour were made of bronze. They wore helmets and carried round shields. They had armour on their bodies and legs. They fought with long spears and short swords. Roman soldiers were called legionaries. Each legionary wore an iron helmet with a neck guard and carried a curved wooden shield. His armour was made from iron plates. A legionary fought with a short iron sword and two throwing spears called javelins.

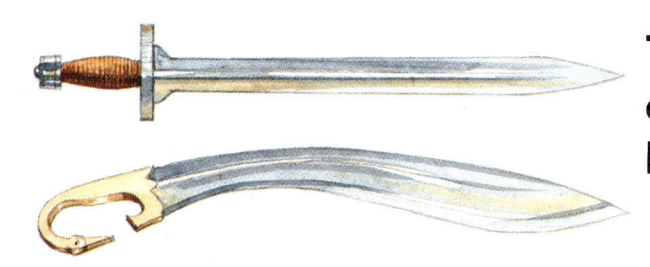

Two types of swords carried by Greek hoplites.

Viking warriors

The Vikings were fierce fighters. About 1,000 years ago, they sailed their longships from Scandinavia to raid other countries. They wore iron helmets which had special face guards and carried round wooden shields. Some Vikings wore mail shirts. These were made from lots of small iron rings linked together. Their favourite weapons were swords and long-handled axes.

11

The knight

A servant called a squire helped a knight to dress.

12

During the Middle Ages, knights dressed in full armour and mounted on powerful horses were the most feared fighters. Knights fought with swords, maces and long spears called lances. A knight wore a mail skirt, a padded tunic with patches of mail sewn on and armour on his feet and legs. Breast plates and back plates covered his body. Arm pieces and gloves called gauntlets covered his arms.

The squire checked all the straps and laces.

Archers

Archers were soldiers who fought with bows and arrows. In the Middle Ages, English archers used longbows made from yew tree wood which was very springy. An archer needed skill and strength to pull the bowstring and fire an arrow. The metal-tipped arrows could pierce armour and kill a fully armoured knight 200m (223yd) away.

Yew tree wood

A longbow and arrow. Arrows were about 0.9m (3ft) long.

A longbow archer could fire twelve arrows a minute.

The crossbow was powerful but took a long time to load. The archer pulled the cord with a hook on his belt.

Nut **Cord**

Trigger

Crossbow arrows were called bolts or quarrels

Knives and swords

People have used knives as tools or weapons for thousands of years.

A knife duel in the Wild West. Each fighter holds one end of a scarf between his teeth. He cannot let go until the duel is finished.

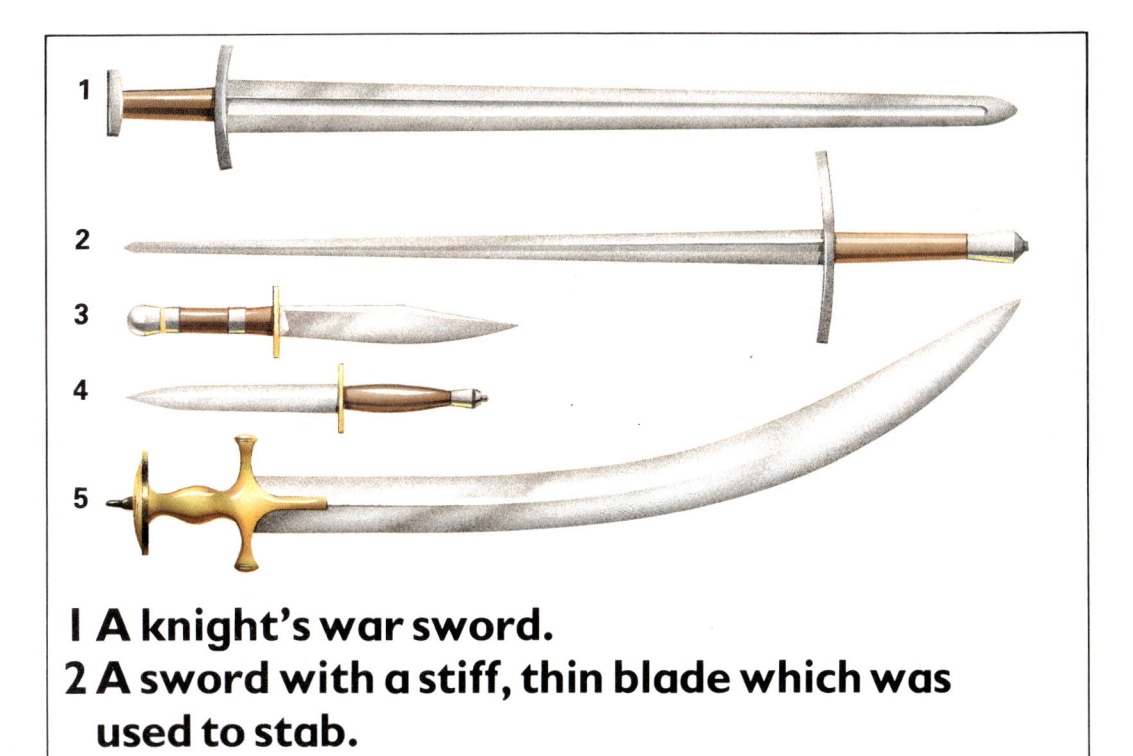

1 A knight's war sword.
2 A sword with a stiff, thin blade which was used to stab.
3 A large hunting knife.
4 A World War II commando knife.
5 An Indian sword called a talwar.

Swords came in all shapes and sizes. Some had straight blades for stabbing. Others were curved and were better for cutting. Some were so big that they had to be held in both hands. Others, like the rapier, were thin and light.

The first cannons

The first cannons in Europe were made in the 1300s. They used gunpowder to fire arrows or solid balls of stone or iron.

A cannon being used in the American Civil War (1861-5).

A modern tank. Its automatic guns can shoot down a plane which is too far away for the gunners to see.

Later cannons were mounted on wheels so they could be moved easily. They fired exploding shells which were filled with bullets. Modern cannons are called artillery. They can hit targets many miles away.

Pistols

Pistols are guns which can be held in one hand. The first pistol was made during the 1500s. Most early pistols could fire only one shot.

Fighting a duel with pistols in about 1800.

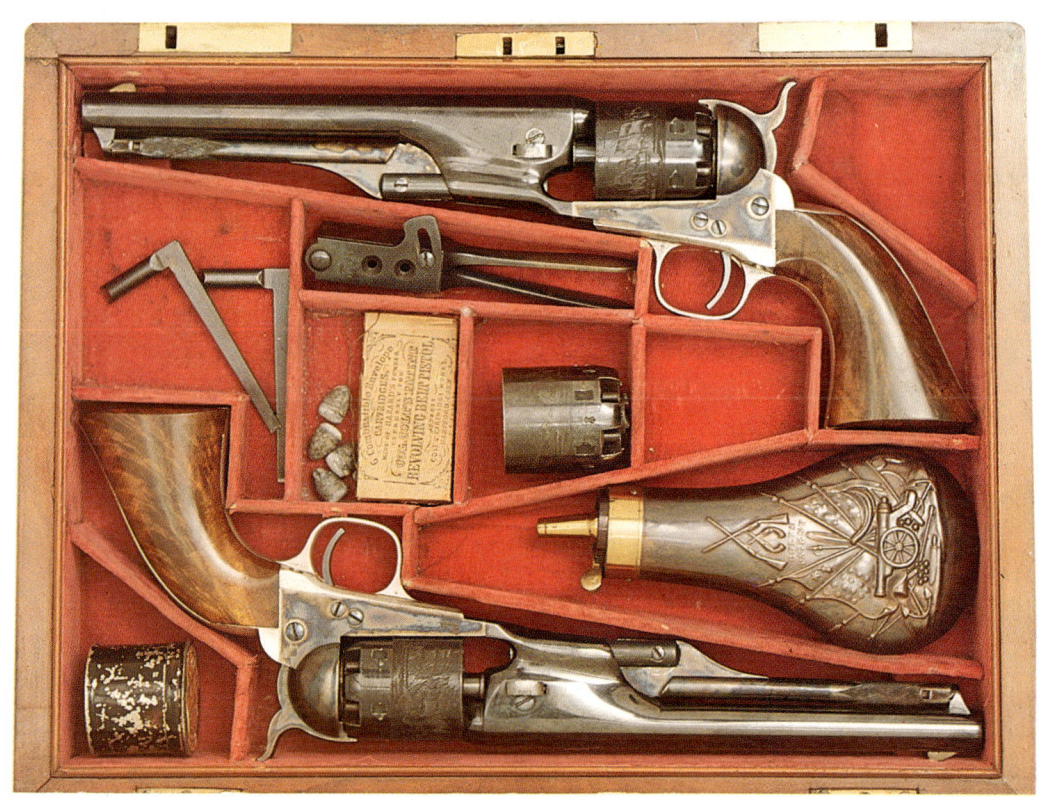

A pair of six-shot Colt revolvers.

In 1836, an American gunmaker called Samuel Colt invented the revolver. This was a pistol which could fire five or six shots. The cartridges were held in a cylinder which revolved. A modern pistol can hold up to fifteen cartridges in its magazine.

Rifles

Loading a musket.

Early gun barrels were smooth tubes. The bullet did not fit very tightly inside. When fired, the bullet wobbled as it moved along the barrel and often missed its target. Gunmakers began to cut spiral grooves, called rifling, on the inside of the barrel. As the bullet travelled along the barrel, the rifling made it spin. The spin made the bullet fly straight through the air.

A Winchester repeating rifle with a lever action.

Muskets had to be loaded through the open end of the barrel. Gunpowder was poured in and then a bullet was rammed down on top of it. the invention of metal cartridges meant that repeating rifles could be made. Cartridges hold a firing cap, gunpowder and a bullet in one case. Repeating rifles carry several cartridges in a magazine. Each cartridge is taken from the magazine and loaded into the rifle by a lever or a bolt.

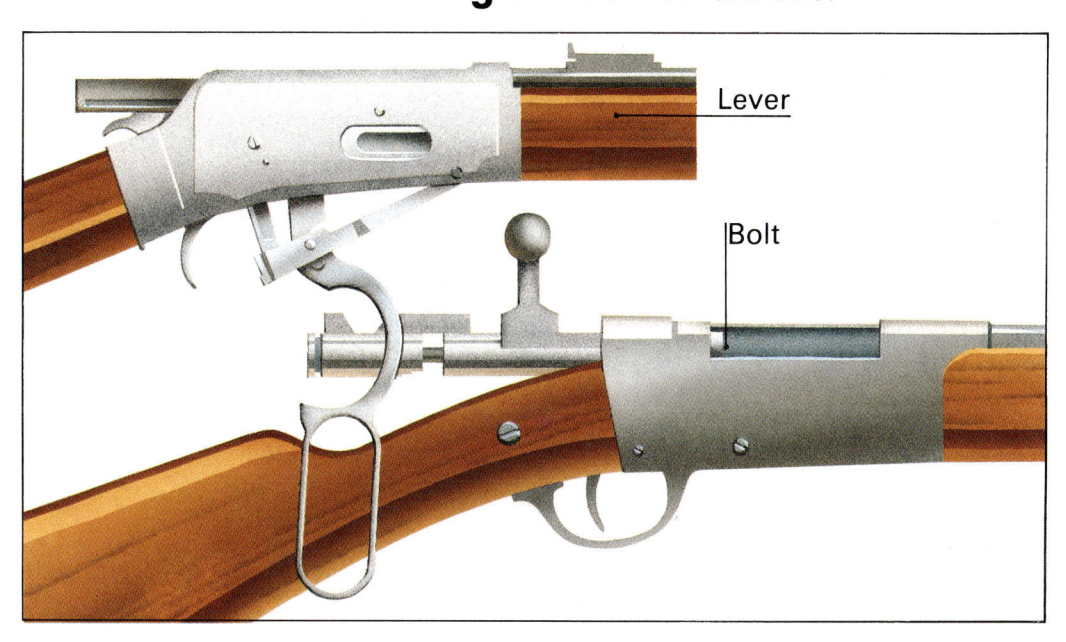

Lever

Bolt

Machine guns

A German machine gun used in World War II. One person fired it and another guided the cartridge belt.

Machine guns will go on firing for as long as the trigger is pressed or until they run out of cartridges. Machine gun cartridges are fed in by a belt. As each cartridge is fired, gas is produced. Some of this gas is used to work the moving parts which fire the next cartridge.

Submachine guns and self-loading rifles work in the same way as machine guns, but they are light enough to be used by a single soldier and the cartridges are fed in from a magazine. A submachine gun can be fitted with a long knife called a bayonet on th end of its barrel.

Magazine

Two AK47 submachine guns. Notice the curved magazines.

The modern soldier

Modern soldiers use many other weapons apart from guns. They can throw small bombs, called grenades. They can carry and fire rockets or even guided missiles. Modern soldiers often wear steel or plastic helmets and special body armour. These protect them from bullets and metal bomb splinters.

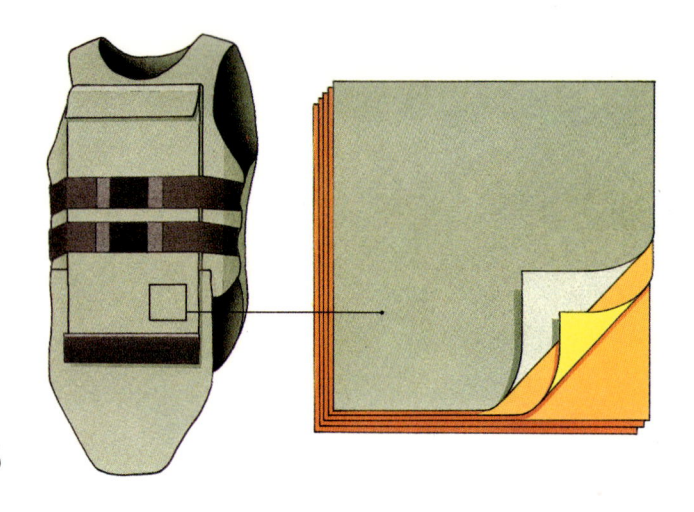

Modern plastic body armour is light and strong.

This soldier is wearing plastic armour under his uniform.

Unusual weapons

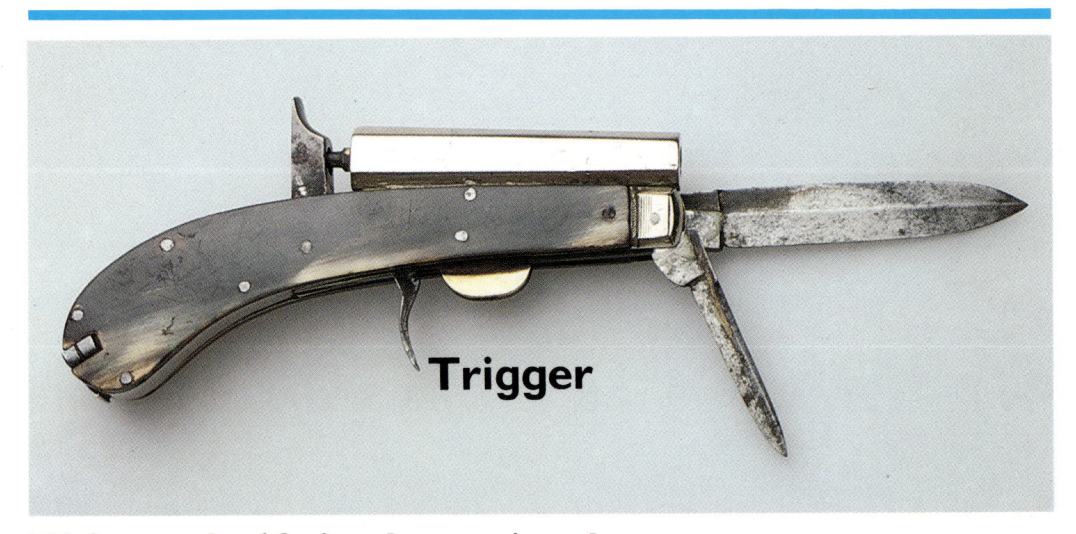

Trigger

This penknife is also a pistol. The trigger folds away when it is not being used.

Some weapons look unusual because they have more than one use. One example is a whip with a pistol hidden in its handle. Some hunters carried swords with pistols fitted to the blades. If they were attacked, the hunters then had two ways of defending themselves.

Some weapons were disguised. The swordstick looked like an ordinary walking stick but had a sword blade hidden inside.

Some unusual knives
1 A kris from Malaya.
2 A kukri from Nepal.
3 A pichangatti from India.

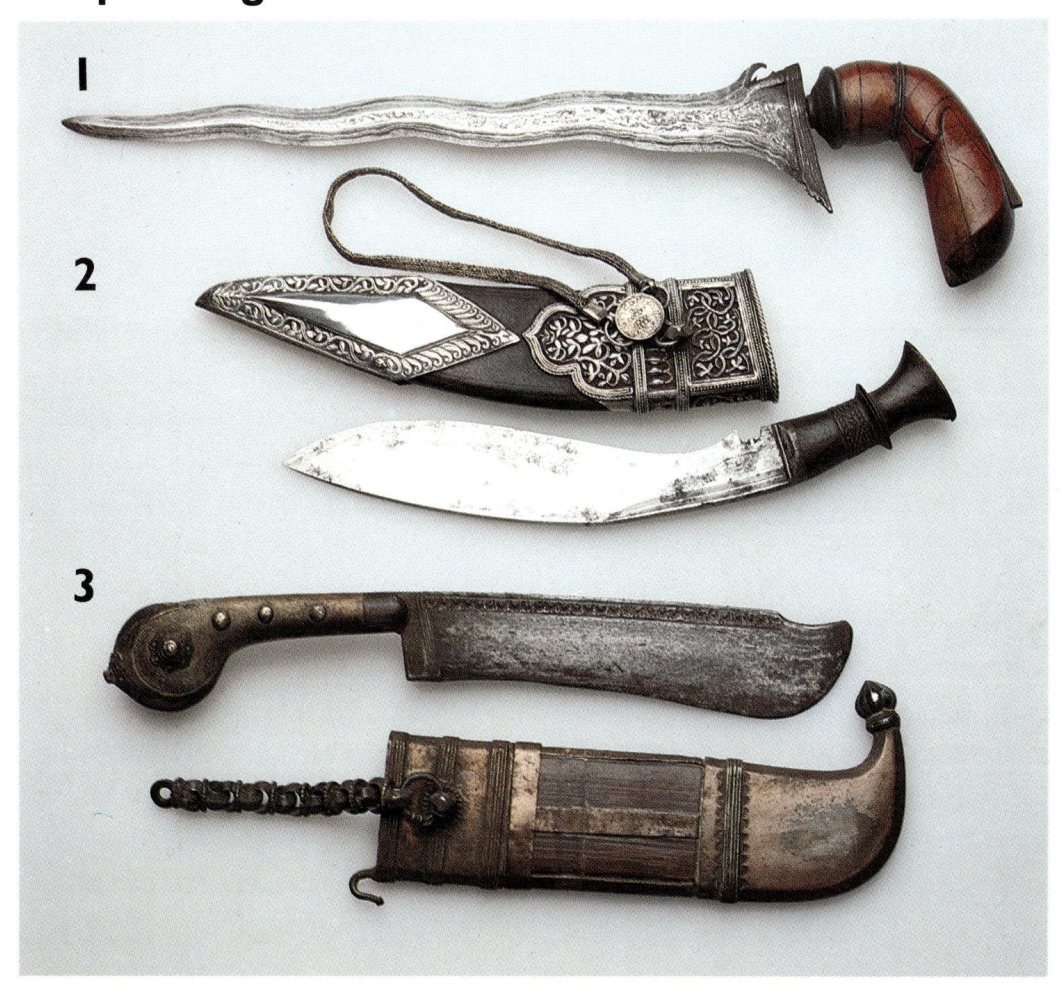

Arms and armour facts

The oldest known weapon is a wooden spear found in Essex in 1911. It is over 200,000 years old.

The oldest army in the world is the Swiss Guard in the Vatican City. It was started in about 1400 and now has 83 members.

The earliest guns were built in about 1250 in China and North Africa.

The biggest guns ever built were German. Two of them were used in World War II. Each weighed 1,344 tonnes and was 42.9m (141ft) long. They could fire 8½ tonne shells as far as 47km (29 miles). Each needed 1,500 soldiers to operate it.

The armour of a Roman legionary could be folded up for carrying on the march.

Armour is not as heavy as it looks. A knight in full armour could move about easily, but it was hot and stuffy inside the metal suit.

Some armour was so heavy that knights had to be lifted on to their horses by a special crane. If knights fell over they could not get to their feet without help.

In the 1600s, a swordsman often fought with a sword in one hand and a dagger in the other. He would use the dagger to catch his opponent's sword. The dagger was called a "main gauche" which is French for "left hand".

Modern rifles can be fitted with night sights which help a soldier to see and hit a target even in darkness. Another type of sight shines a laser beam spot on to the target.

Glossary

Here is the meaning of some of the words used in this book:

Barrel
A metal tube on a gun along which the bullet travels.

Cannon
A large gun. It was loaded from the open end of the barrel. Gunpowder was poured in and a cannon ball rammed down on top.

Cartridge
A case made of plastic or metal which contains bullet, gunpowder and firing cap. Cartridges are loaded into rifles, machine guns and pistols.

Firing cap
A small cap in the end of a cartridge which is struck by a firing pin to make the gunpowder explode.

Flint
A hard stone which flakes easily leaving a sharp edge. Used by Stone Age people to make tools and weapons. Also used to make the spark to fire a musket.

Guided missile
A rocket-powered shell which can be steered on to its target.

Lever action
A type of repeating rifle where the cartridges are lifted from the magazine by moving a lever up and down.

Magazine
A box inside (or attached to) a rifle, submachine gun or pistol, which holds a number of cartridges. The word also means a store for gunpowder.

Index

Archers 14-15
Armour 13, 14, 26, 27, 30
Arrow 5, 7, 14, 15, 18
Axe 5, 10

Bows 14-15
Bronze 4, 5, 9
Bullets 19, 22, 23, 26

Cannon 18-19, 31
Cartridge 21, 23, 24, 25, 31
Colt revolver 21

Egyptians 6-7

Firing cap 23, 31
Flint 5, 31

Grenades 26
Guided missiles 27, 31
Gun powder 18, 23

Helmets 9, 10, 26

Iron 5, 9, 10

Knight 12-13, 30
Knives 5, 16-17, 25, 28, 29

Lever action 23, 31

Mace 13
Machine gun 24-5, 30
Magzine 21, 23, 25, 31

Mail 10, 13
Muskets 23

Pistols 20-1, 28

Rapier 17, 31
Rifle 22-3, 30

Self-loading rifle 25, 31
Shell 19, 30, 31
Shields 7, 9, 10
Spear 5, 7, 9, 13, 30
Swords 7, 9, 10, 13, 16-17, 28, 29

Tank 19